A GUIDE TO EVANGELISM

A GUIDE TO

Evangelism

Dan DeWitt, Editor

GUIDE BOOK NO. *004*

———

To my mom,
the most natural evangelist
I've ever known.

Dan DeWitt

———

A GUIDE TO EVANGELISM

TABLE OF CONTENTS

—

INTRODUCTION

—

EVANGELISM: AN INTRODUCTION

Dan DeWitt

Many Christians, according to Russell D. Moore, think about evangelism like they think about flossing. They know they should do it more often – and they even feel guilty when they're reminded of it – but they think of it as an optional discipline.

Such a laissez-faire approach to evangelism is certainly foreign to Scripture. Charles Haddon Spurgeon went so far as to say that this sort of attitude is antithetical to the gospel itself. "Have you no wish for others to be saved?" Spurgeon asked. "Then you're not saved yourself, be sure of that!"

Perhaps the metaphor of food is a more appropriate way to view our responsibility to share the gospel. Sri Lankan evangelist D.T. Niles said that evangelism is simply, "One beggar telling another beggar where he can find bread."

We must recognize that lost people are unlike hungry people in that they are unaware of their need for spiritual bread. Our task would be much easier if everyone sensed the hunger pangs of their sacred starvation. For that matter, our task would be easier if we as believers would better nurture an appetite for spreading the faith by sharing the gospel. Too often, we can be guilty of being gospel hoarders and simultaneously spiritually malnourished. If we hide the gospel away for our families, and ourselves, the result will be an evangelistic anorexia that fails to convince the watching world that we have found the source of supreme satisfaction. God help us.

This little book is designed to help you cultivate your craving to see "grace extend to more and more people" so that it "may increase thanksgiving, to the glory of God" (2 Cor 4:15). If you finish this guide book and still see the Great Commission like the unfortunate duty to floss accompanied by a scolding from a well-intentioned hygienist, then we have failed. And so have you.

It's our goal that the following pages serve you by fanning your passion for the glory of God. And it's our prayer that each chapter will provide some helpful resources for sharing the gospel with specific people groups, both as individuals and churches. We confess up front our complete reliance upon the gospel as the exclusive power of God for saving sinners (Rom 1:16).

Of this we need not be ashamed.

So, since you own a copy of God's Word, even if you had never stumbled upon this little book, you already have all you need to share your faith sufficiently. So why publish this book?

We understand the perennial need for the scriptural reminder that sharing the gospel is the joyful duty of every believer. And we want to provide some insights from leaders who have spent significant time evangelizing different groups like Mormons, Muslims, skeptics and even lost persons who might sit next to you in your church pew on Sunday mornings.

Take what you can that's helpful. Feel free to disregard the rest. And as you read, pray that God will give you a boundless passion to see the kingdom spread like wildfire from house to house and shore to shore.

Too often, we can be guilty of being gospel hoarders and simultaneously spiritually malnourished.

Jesus once told a parable that likened the kingdom of heaven to a great wedding banquet (Matt 22:1-14). After the original invitations were rejected, the servants went out into the main streets and invited everyone they could find to return with them to the feast. The surprised guests were welcomed at the party.

Jesus also told a series of "lost stories" in Luke 15. One story is about a lost sheep. The second is about a lost coin. The third is about a lost son. All three stories end with a party and illustrate the fact that there is great rejoicing in heaven over one sinner who repents.

All of these stories end with scenes of food, feasts, celebrations and parties to describe God's response to people coming to saving faith. If we look at evangelism like dental floss, we have missed the point in a bigger way than we may care to realize. God entrusts the Christian with the divine duty – the magnificent mandate – to spread the invitation to the eternal celebration of God's redeeming love.

May this resource encourage you to hit the streets in like manner to tell hungry beggars where they can find the bread of life. For whoever encounters Jesus in saving faith will never hunger nor thirst again (John 6:35). Let the party begin. ∞

—

FOR THE
CHURCH

—

THEOLOGICAL INCENTIVES
FOR EVANGELISM

Chad Brand

A s in other areas of Christian practice, worship, prayer, preaching and counseling, evangelism needs to be undergirded by a theological reflection on just what it is we are doing and why. This is because, as R.B. Kuiper puts it, "Evangelism has its roots in eternity."

In this chapter, I won't address the doctrine of salvation directly. Instead, I will address the theological issues that compel Christians to "go." In so doing, I will touch on some of the important issues that relate to the doctrine of salvation itself, but an examination of the issues related to a thorough doctrine of salvation will have to be sought elsewhere.

God Compels Us

The place to begin articulating a theology of evangelism is the love of God. There is good reason that John 3:16 is such a beloved text of Scripture. In the first four chapters of John's Gospel, though the world lies in darkness and wickedness, God loves it. Charles Wesley expressed the idea poetically by asking, "Amazing love, how can it be, that thou my God shouldst die for me?"

God's love is not great because the world is so large, but because the people who dwell in it are so bad. God calls on his people to be co-lovers of the world with him, and in so doing to extend the love of God to those who have not yet recognized and experienced it in a saving manner. We share the gospel because God loves the world.

Our theology of evangelism also entails the belief that God has chosen to save a great multitude of persons. Not everyone who reads this will agree on how to articulate the doctrine of election, but we can all agree that "He chose us in him [Christ] before the foundation of the world, that we should be holy and blameless before him" (Eph 1:4). The result of this election is that a great multitude will be saved, a multitude of "myriads of myriads and thousands of thousands" (Rev 5:11).

When we think of God's electing purpose and its relation to evangelism, we should recognize that we are about the task of calling to salvation all of those whom the Lord has known to be his from the foundation of the world (Eph 1:3). It was this truth, among others, that compelled one of the founders of the modern mission movement, William Carey, to work for seven years before he saw a single convert in India; he was convinced that God had people in that land who were his own. Election ought not merely be a debate point, but a central feature of our theology of

God's love is not great because the world is so large, but because the people who dwell in it are so bad.

evangelism, even though it might function somewhat differently depending on how we construe it. We need to expend more energy in preaching for the chosen of the Lord than in debating the doctrine in coffee houses.

Why is it that people need to be saved? Most foundationally, lost people do not willingly glorify God or submit to the lordship of Christ. The glory of God and the lordship of Christ are the two consuming passions of Scripture's authors. God created the world to display his glory (Ps 19), and in his resurrection Christ was declared with power to be both Son of God and Lord of the universe (Acts 2:36; Rom 1:3-4).

In evangelism, and what results from evangelism, whether in our own neighborhood or around the globe, we bring the greatest glory to God and extend his Son's lordship.

It is not the winning of souls alone that does this, but also what it entails and what follows: the bowing of knees to the Lord and the initiation of a life of worship for those so saved. As the Dutch pastor, statesman and theologian, Abraham Kuyper put it, "There is not one square inch in the whole domain of our human existence over which Christ, who is sovereign over all, does not cry, 'Mine.'" That domain includes the lives of those who do not yet know their sovereign.

People Compel Us

Evangelism also demands an understanding of the spiritual state of those whom we evangelize. In order for lost people to glorify God rightly and submit to the lordship of Christ, they need forgiveness of sins. We evangelize because people are lost in sins and their only hope is the gospel of Jesus Christ. Their problem is doubly bad: they are lost, but do not know it. The apostle Paul depicts the response of unbelievers at the time of the second coming as one of total shock. They will say, "Peace and

> We need to expend more energy in preaching for the chosen of the Lord than in debating the doctrine in coffee houses.

In order for lost people to glorify God rightly and submit to the lordship of Christ, they need forgiveness of sins.

security," before he comes like a thief in the night (1 Thess 5:1-4).

Lost people do not know their peril. Some recognize that they have "problems," and they may employ some self-help, or "religion," or attempt to make themselves pleasing to God through philanthropy or moral improvement. But the gospel makes clear that such efforts are to no avail.

Cornelius Van Til once illustrated such efforts by comparing them to a man made of water, trying to get out of a vat of water, by climbing up a ladder made of water. The analogy, someone might say, is ridiculous – but so is the belief that one can save oneself. The gospel message articulated by Paul in Romans 1-4 and in Ephesians 1-2 renders that entirely clear, as do many other passages.

Humans also have a fundamental need for a conversion experience. The greatest of all evangelism texts makes this abundantly clear:

> Go, therefore, and make disciples of all nations, baptizing them in the name of the Father and of the Son and of the Holy Spirit, teaching them to observe everything I have commanded you. And remember, I am with you always, to the end of the age (Matt 28:19-20).

We must make disciples, and this most often happens with a gospel encounter and a resultant experience of repentance and faith.

Curiously, such a theology of evangelism was absent from most of the church for much of its history. Even with the Reformers' recovery of the doctrine of justification by faith, they often did not call for a "crisis of faith," or a specific moment when a person became a disciple. They catechized their children (nothing wrong with that), and believed that the elect among their children (hopefully all of them) would find justification. But it was Anabaptists like Menno Simons and Conrad Grebel in that period who first urged people to repent and be baptized.

They were followed in the next century by many Puritans, who spent years "preparing" their children for conversion, so that they might be capable of relating a genuine conversion, become "visible saints" and enter into the full covenant of the church. Then, in the next century it was the revivalists Jonathan Edwards, and especially George Whitefield, who took that to the next level and preached to large numbers, calling upon them to experience the new birth.

A theology of evangelism must emphasize the conversion experience, even if there are some in the church who do not remember their moment of conversion; if they are saved today, there was a time when their discipleship was "made."

The Task Compels Us

What is the primary means by which the gospel is set forth? The primary means of evangelism is Scripture. Paul asks, "How then will they call on him in whom they have not believed? And how are they to believe in him of whom they have never heard? And how are they to hear without someone preaching? And how are they to preach unless they are sent? As it is written, 'How beautiful are the feet of those who preach the good news!'" (Rom 10:14-15). The "him" in whom they must believe is the "him" of the Gospel narratives, the one predicted and anticipated in the whole Old Testament, the one explained and commented on in Acts and Epistles, and the one who appears in all his radiant glory in the book of Revelation.

> The "him" in whom they must believe is the "him" of the Gospel narratives, the one predicted and anticipated in the whole Old Testament, the one explained and commented on in Acts and Epistles.

D. Martyn Lloyd-Jones asserted, "Preaching is the greatest and highest and most glorious calling to which anyone can ever be called." He was not thereby exalting the ministry to a higher vocation than, say, a butcher or a baker, but was saying that proclaiming the Word is the greatest thing any of us can do. And it can be done by those who are not ordained "clergy." It is in fact the task of all Christians (1 Pet 3:15).

One of the reasons we need to address this issue of the power of God's Word to bring lost people to Christ is that so many in our day seek to win people to Christianity by means of entertainment and by resorting only to rhetorical and emotional appeals without sufficient gospel and biblical content. God has promised to use Scripture to dissect the thoughts and intentions of the heart and thereby to change our lives (Heb 4:12), not entertainment or emotional and content-less appeals.

Eternity Compels Us

Finally, the doctrine that compels us to share the gospel as much and as widely as we can is the return of our Lord. We do not know when he will return, of course, but it could be very soon, so we want to do our part to extend Christ's

> We want to do our part to extend Christ's active lordship into as many lives as possible in the time we have.

active lordship into as many lives as possible in the time we have.

J. I. Packer, in addressing the question of how we know we are doing biblical evangelism, says this: "The way to tell whether in fact you are evangelizing is not to ask whether conversions are known to have resulted from your witness. It is to ask whether you are faithfully making known the gospel message." What is that gospel message? It is that Jesus died to save sinners, shedding his blood on the cross as our sacrifice and our substitute. What is the response to the gospel message? It is repentance and faith, faith that Jesus has done all that is necessary to save us. Put your hope in him, the one who is coming soon, remembering that after he comes, judgment follows. ∞

PREACHING THAT PROPAGATES

Brian Payne

I had the privilege of playing football at the University of Alabama. It was an opportunity that I wouldn't trade for anything. However, if anyone thinks that college football is all about the excitement that takes place on autumn afternoons, they are highly naïve. Most of a college football player's time is spent in the drudgery of offseason workouts.

The Kingdom of Wingo

While at Alabama, my strength and conditioning coach was Rich Wingo, a former linebacker for Alabama and the Green Bay Packers. He is the toughest human being I have ever encountered, and I'm convinced that he must have played without a helmet. If you survived a Wingo offseason conditioning workout, it was a point of great satisfaction.

But Wingo also knew that, no matter how great a motivator he was, he needed incentives to encourage the players to push the limits of their endurance. So, in the spring of 1989, he told us that, at the end of winter workouts, he would hand out "Bama Pride" workout shirts to those who excelled in the offseason conditioning program.

To my delight, I was one of five players who earned the "Bama Pride" shirt. Possessing this shirt set you apart as a devoted and disciplined disciple of the Wingo kingdom.

But then came a day of reckoning. We were in a spring training scrimmage in our indoor practice facility. Then the fullback came out to block me and went for my knee. My knee hyperextended, putting me in extreme pain, so the trainers pulled me to the side and placed ice on my knee.

Five minutes into my injury, Wingo saw me. He said, "BP, get on the stationary bike and peddle at 1500 RPM's." I knew this was a good time to reason with him, so I said, "Coach Wingo, I just injured my knee and what you're asking would be a challenge for two healthy legs."

He looked at me and said, "BP, get off the bike." "Ah," I thought, "he does have a heart." But at that moment, he started pushing the bike and told me to follow. He pushed it outside, where it was sleeting. He then looked at me and said, "Now maybe you can get it to 1500 RPM's." I decided that he needed to be reasoned with again. So I said, "Coach Wingo, if I can't peddle this hard in 72 degrees, I will probably have a harder time peddling in 35 degrees." He looked at me and said, "BP, lift up your arms." As I did, he pulled that "Bama Pride" shirt off my back and said, "you don't deserve this anymore." At that point, I started peddling, because I didn't know what else he might pull off.

Wingo's method was effective. He knew how to motivate and push you beyond your perceived limits. We knew the terms of his kingdom, and we knew the consequences of not meeting those terms. But, in his kingdom, our inner attitude toward him was irrelevant. As long as we showed outward respect to him and met his terms and demands, love or hate toward him was utterly inconsequential.

That is, in a nutshell, the difference between human kingdoms and the kingdom of God. In the former, outward conformity, apparent submission and external allegiance and obedience are all that matters. But in God's kingdom, why we do what we do is as important as what we do. This is what Paul means when he writes that, all that we do is to be done with "sincerity of heart, fearing the Lord," and "heartily, as for the Lord" (Col 3:22-23).

It's important, when we think about the kingdom, that we know what it is and how it erupts into the present age.

The Kingdom of God: God's Reign over All of Creation Through the Messiah

Scripture begins with the announcement that God, as creator, is the sovereign king of the universe. In this sense, the entire universe is God's kingdom, and he alone is to be worshipped

> The entire universe is God's kingdom, and he alone is to be worshipped and obeyed.

and obeyed. Indeed, "The Lord has established his throne in the heavens, and his kingdom rules over all" (Ps 103:19). It is undeniable that the Lord reigns (Ps 93:1; 97:1; 99:1).

But if God's kingdom is already universal and comprehensive, how do we make sense of Jesus' prayer that God's kingdom come (Lk 11:2)? Jesus is referring to something new – a need brought on by human sin, rebellion and death.

Before the fall, God created a world that he described as "very good." Yet now, in light of a human revolt, God's rule over creation is rejected by humankind. Consequently, we now stand under God's sentence of condemnation, guilt and death (Gen 2:16-17; Rom 3:23; 6:23).

It's at this juncture that the Old Testament makes a critical distinction between the sovereign reign of God over the entire creation and the coming of his saving reign, by which he makes all things right. This salvation plan becomes the theme of the Bible and of redemptive history. Israel's hope becomes a messianic redeemer who will set creation right – to usher in the saving reign of God. This is the kingdom that Jesus tells us to pray for – a kingdom that will dispel all sin and rebellion and include a redeemed people who serve as his vice-regents over a new heaven and new earth.

In the Old Testament, this hope for a messianic redeemer is announced by the prophets. This redeemer, who is mysteriously both "Mighty God" and a descendent of David (Isa 9:6-7), will have "dominion from sea to sea and from the River to the ends of the earth" (Ps 72:8). To say it another way, God's plan was to glorify himself by establishing his saving reign over all of creation through the agency of the Davidic Messiah.

The New Testament proclaims that, in Jesus Christ, the long-awaited kingdom has come and, with him, the deathblow to the rule of sin, death and the devil. In the cross, resurrection and ascension of Jesus Christ, this divine plan has been actualized and God's saving reign has moved into the world to reconstitute, reconcile and renew a people and the cosmos. Because of Christ's victory, the kingdom goal is accomplished. There is nothing that can or need be added. God in Christ has overcome the alienation that characterized fallen creation.

Yet not everyone recognizes or submits to the reign of Christ. This brings us to the means of the kingdom. The kingdom is brought about by God through Christ by the Holy Spirit. Yet, as the Bible makes clear, God employs human means.

The New Testament proclaims that, in Jesus Christ, the long-awaited kingdom has come and, with him, the deathblow to the rule of sin, death and the devil.

The Means of the Kingdom: The Preaching of the Gospel of the Kingdom

The primary means by which God advances the kingdom of Christ is Spirit-empowered preaching. The Puritan preacher, Cotton Mather, said that the great purpose of preaching is to "restore the throne and dominion of God in the souls of men."

The New Testament makes it clear that the preacher heralds the gospel of the kingdom (e.g., Mt 3:2; 4:7; 9:35; Lk 8:1; 9:2).

The gospel of the kingdom is this: there is one God, and there is one mediator between God and men, the man Christ Jesus, who gave himself as a ransom for sinners (1 Tim 2:5-6). This is the message for which Paul says he was appointed a preacher (1 Tim 2:7). Paul, elsewhere, summarizes the message this way: that the Savior Christ Jesus abolished death and brought life and immortality to light through the gospel (2 Tim 1:10). Again, Paul adds that it is for this proclaimed message he was appointed a preacher (2 Tim 1:11).

Unlike many sermons today that are preached in the "imperative mode" (commands), the message of the kingdom is primarily in the "indicative mode." And that great declaration can be summarized by the announcement that the kingdom has arrived because Christ Jesus, who conquered sin, death and the devil through his cross and resurrection now reigns and rules.

Preaching must focus on the announcement of God's victory in Jesus Christ through his cross and resurrection (the indicative). This is nothing less than the gospel of the kingdom. Yet, at the same time, preaching must demand a response. Sinners do not enter this kingdom without coming on God's terms – and those terms are repentance

> Paul summarizes the message this way: that the Savior Christ Jesus abolished death and brought life and immortality to light through the gospel.

and faith. This is seen with the apostle Paul, who went about "proclaiming the kingdom" (Acts 20:25). Yet, preaching of the kingdom requires a human response. Hence, Paul's "testifying ... of repentance toward God and of faith in our Lord Jesus Christ" (20:21).

Paul's model of preaching the kingdom and the terms of the kingdom leads us to the final section of this chapter. In this section, we look at some of the final words we ever hear from the apostle – and, not surprisingly, it's a call to his preacher protégé, Timothy, to preach. What we see is that the message is consistent elsewhere in the New Testament. Indeed, the passage ties our entire discussion together.

2 Timothy 4:1-2

In 2 Timothy, the apostle gives to Timothy some last words before the apostle's subsequent martyrdom. In chapter 3, Paul warns Timothy that in the "last days" times will be "difficult."

He proceeds to list 18 items that characterize these times. The list begins and ends with words expressing misdirected love, suggesting that misdirected love is the fundamental problem with lost people. That is, people will be "lovers of self" and "lovers

Misdirected love is the fundamental problem with lost people.

of pleasure rather than God." All the vices that fall between these two characteristics are the fruit of this misdirected love. In 3:5, the apostle implies that he hasn't been primarily referring to those outside the church, but those who have "the appearance of godliness, but denying its power" (3:5); that is, professing believers within the church.

Paul then applies that description to the particular case of false teachers in Timothy's situation. He then reminds Timothy that gospel ministry in this context is costly and will lead to persecution (2 Tim 3:10-12). In fact, it will only get worse (2 Tim 3:13).

It is at this point, many church consultants in our culture would say, that Paul needs to be innovative with Timothy. Timothy needs to do something novel and relevant, or employ effective business and marketing practices in order to reach a culture that is increasingly secular.

But Paul understands that the situation is hopeless without God's Word. It's only this authority that can change lovers of self and pleasure to those who are lovers of God. Consequently, Paul lays out the strongest defense in all of Scripture for the sufficiency of Scripture in ministry. Because it is the very "God-breathed" Word from God, it is sufficient for salvation and sanctification. Hence, the Word is sufficient for preaching (2 Tim 4:1-2).

Paul's encouragement to Timothy in 2 Timothy 4 is given in the presence of God and Christ, with distinct reference to Jesus' return, kingdom and judgeship.

It is in the context of this hope that Paul exhorts Timothy to "preach the Word." In light

> In 2 Timothy 3:16-17, Paul lays out the strongest defense in all of Scripture for the sufficiency of Scripture in ministry.

of the pending consummation of the kingdom, the minister is to "preach." Furthermore, by placing this command first in verse 2, Paul makes it clear that this is the central mark of Christian ministry. This is seen also in the fact that this command to preach is amplified by the second imperative, "be ready in season and out of season," and by the prepositional phrase, "with complete patience and teaching," at the end of the verse.

This command is followed by four transformational objectives: reprove, rebuke, exhort and teach. In other words, the gospel of the kingdom demands a response. In light of Christ's appearing, kingdom and impending judgment, sinners must come to him on his terms, and the preacher's central responsibility is to set forth those terms.

Teaching concerns itself with "sound doctrine in accordance with the glorious gospel of the blessed God" (1 Tim 1:10-11). Accordingly, it is by the "teaching" of the realities of the triumph of the kingdom of Christ that the preacher is able to reprove, rebuke and exhort.

This brings us to the theme of our chapter: preaching that propagates. The American Heritage Dictionary defines

Christ's kingdom requires heartfelt fidelity, faithfulness and loyalty.

"propagate" as "to cause to extend to a broader area or larger number, spread to make widely known; publicize."

What do we extend and spread? It's simple: the saving reign of Jesus Christ. As sinners are converted to Christ, his saving reign spreads, accomplishing the divine purpose to spread his reign "from sea to sea ... to the ends of the earth" (Ps 72:8). Furthermore, as Jesus' dominion is extended to the ends of the earth, the divine purpose of having the whole earth filled with God's glory is achieved. This is God's kingdom plan: to glorify himself by establishing his reign over all of creation through his Messiah.

This occurs in the present age as sinners are converted to Jesus and his rule. In so doing, God "qualifies" these converts (Col 1:12) to "share in the inheritance" of the LORD's anointed, who through his victory is given the "ends of the earth" as his possession (Ps 2:1-8). Indeed, God delivers these converts "from the domain of darkness and transfers" them "to the kingdom of his beloved Son in whom" they "have redemption, the forgiveness of sins" (Col 1:13-14).

Conclusion

Earthly kings and kingdoms do not require, nor can they require, their subjects to love them. In my case, coach Wingo found it inconsequential whether we loved him or not. He merely demanded outward allegiance. But Christ's kingdom is not of this world (John 18:36). This kingdom requires heartfelt fidelity, faithfulness and loyalty because Christ is our king by virtue of creation and his sufferings, death and resurrection on behalf of sinners. Indeed, Jesus "gave himself for our sins to deliver us from the present evil age, according to the will of our God and Father" (Gal 1:4). Hence, he is worthy of all glory, honor, praise, thanksgiving and love.

The only message that will provoke that kind of heartfelt response is the message of the kingdom. As the preacher proclaims the gospel of the kingdom and the terms of that kingdom – repentance and faith – the saving reign of Christ is propagated. ✞

EVANGELISM AND
CHURCH DISCIPLINE

Denny Burk

A number of years ago, I was teaching a Bible study at a large church. After finishing my lesson, a woman approached me in tears. She wanted to know how she could possibly be a faithful wife to a husband who was not being faithful to her. Her husband was a successful businessman and claimed to be a Christian, but he was not walking with the Lord. Even though I was a guest teacher, I decided that I would try to reach out to this wayward husband and see if I could help reconcile these two who seemed on the precipice of divorce.

We met at a coffee shop for our first meeting. I asked him what was going on and why his wife was so unhappy. He admitted to drinking pretty heavily and to staying out late in bars almost every weeknight. He also confessed that flirting with other women was a regular feature of his nightly carousing. I suspect that he was being unfaithful to his wife – although I never had any proof, there was enough smoke to suggest a fire.

He also claimed to be a Christian. I confronted him on this point and told him that his life did not match his confession and that the Bible offers no assurance to such people (1 John 2:4-6). I was as candid with the guy as I knew how to be. I warned him that he wasn't just in danger of losing his family. He was in danger of losing his soul.

He had a distorted view of what the Christian life was all about. He believed that a person could make a profession of faith and then live in any way he or she pleased while still having assurance of salvation. Following Christ and being saved by Christ

didn't necessarily go together for this guy. He considered himself saved even though he knew that he was unrepentant of the destruction he was heaping on his wife and children.

After confronting him over a series of meetings, he agreed that he needed to change his ways in order to do right by the Lord and his family. I recommended some concrete steps of repentance, and he pledged to carry them out. But he never really did. He never repented. Even after I brought another brother from our church along to confront him, he never changed his ways. One night he ended up passed-out drunk in his car, having run into the tree in his neighbor's yard. His wife had to pull him out of the car and drag him into the house before the neighbors woke up.

After that incident, I decided we had done all we could do. Even though it grieved me to admit it, it was past time for the church to get involved. So I took the matter to one of the pastors of the church and laid out the whole situation. I told the pastor, "It is time for the church to intervene in discipline." The pastor could not respond immediately, but wanted more time to think about next steps. When the pastor finally called me back, I couldn't believe the words that came out of his mouth about the possibility of church discipline. He said: "We know what the Bible says, but we just can't do that."

The Necessity of Discipline

Is it really an option for Christians to look at what the Bible teaches about discipline and conclude, "We just can't do that?" If you were to survey the landscape of evangelical churches in America today, by and large, you would find that most churches do, in fact, act as if discipline is optional. In fact, so few churches practice discipline anymore that many church members don't even know what it is. The idea of removing a member from fellowship seems unloving and foreign. It seems out of place in the midst of a culture that prizes tolerance and individual freedom. Yet the New Testament teaches that discipline is by no means optional; it's a distinguishing mark of faithful churches everywhere.

The New Testament's teaching is unambiguous. There comes a time when the church must confront unrepentant sinners and eventually remove them from membership. This removal from membership is what theologians call "excommunication." The entire process of confrontation is called discipline.

What does church discipline have to do with evangelism? Well, everything. Have you ever heard a skeptic say that he could never become a Christian or go to church because "All those people are just a bunch of hypocrites." When churches fail to do redemptive church discipline, that criticism turns out to be right. Discipline is a means by which churches encourage holiness among their membership. It is also a means by which churches distinguish themselves from the world. Christians are to be lights in the midst of darkness. But where discipline fails, churches become darkness in the midst of darkness.

> Christians are to be lights in the midst of darkness. But where discipline fails, churches become darkness in the midst of darkness.

For this reason, both discipline and excommunication are essential ingredients both for the church and for its wider witness to the community.

Two Key Texts

How is church discipline to be carried out in the life of the local church? There are two primary passages in the New Testament that define the practice of church discipline: Matthew 18:15-20 and 1 Corinthians 5:1-13.

MATTHEW 18:15-20

"If your brother sins against you, go and tell him his fault, between you and him alone. If he listens to you, you have gained your brother. But if he does not listen, take one or two others along with you, that every charge may be established by the evidence of two or three witnesses. If he refuses to listen to them, tell it to the church. And if he refuses to listen even to the church, let him be to you as a Gentile and a tax collector. Truly, I say to you, whatever you bind on earth shall be bound in heaven, and whatever you loose on earth shall be loosed in heaven. Again I say to you, if two of you agree on earth about anything they ask, it will be done for them by

The only sin that churches discipline for is unrepentance.

my Father in heaven. For where two or three are gathered in my name, there am I among them."

There is a process that Jesus gives us in this passage. When someone sins against you, you don't go public with it. You go private with it. You confront the person in private and invite him or her to repent. If the person does not respond, then you take someone else with you to invite him or her to repent. If the person doesn't respond to the entreaty of witnesses, then you tell the whole church, which then invites the sinner to repent. If the person doesn't respond to the church, then Jesus commands the whole church to treat the unrepentant sinner as a "Gentile and a tax-gatherer," which is Jesus' way of saying, "Treat the unrepentant like an unbeliever, and excommunicate him or her from the fellowship."

Notice that the only sin that churches discipline for is unrepentance. At any stage in the process outlined above, this discipline process can end if the person sinning would simply "listen" and repent. If that sinner repents, then there is forgiveness and full restoration to fellowship. How many times do we forgive such sinners who repent? In the very next passage, Jesus says that we must forgive them seventy times seven (Matt 18:22). Our forgiveness is unlimited, just like Jesus' is to us.

In 1 Corinthians 5, Paul deals with a man in the Corinthian church who is having an affair with his step mother.

1 CORINTHIANS 5:1-5, 11

It is actually reported that there is sexual immorality among you, and of a kind that is not tolerated even among pagans, for a man has his father's wife. And you are arrogant! Ought you not rather to mourn? Let him who has done this be removed from among you. For though absent in body, I am present in spirit; and as if present, I have already pronounced judgment on the one who did such a thing. When you are assembled in the name of the Lord Jesus and my spirit is present, with the power of our Lord Jesus, you are to deliver this man to Satan for the destruction of the flesh, so that his spirit may be saved in the day of the Lord.

But now I am writing to you not to associate with anyone who bears the name of brother if he is guilty of sexual immorality or greed, or is an idolater, reviler, drunkard, or swindler — not even to eat with such a one.

Notice that, in this passage, Paul has no word of rebuke at all for the two people committing incest. His entire rebuke is against the church for failing to deal with the sinning members: "You have become arrogant, and have not mourned instead, in order that the one who had done this deed might be removed from your midst" (v. 2). Paul has righteous indignation about this situation, but he's mainly angry at the church. Why? Because it is their responsibility under Christ to preserve the purity of the church. Where sin is not dealt with, it spreads (1 Cor 5:6-7). So the unrepentant must be removed in order to protect the spiritual integrity of the church. When a church refuses to remove, it is being "arrogant" and acting like it knows better how to run the church than Christ does.

And so we too are arrogant if we refuse to discipline as Christ has commanded us to discipline.

Failing to discipline compromises the witness of the church.

We don't need to be trigger-happy about excommunicating members; it ought to grieve us deeply whenever unrepentant sin leads to excommunication. But we also must not shrink back when the occasion requires. If a member won't repent, we must obey Christ.

What's at Stake?

What happens when we fail to discipline? Christ's rule in our churches is threatened if we don't obey him in this. When we don't discipline, eventually the church membership becomes made of believers and unbelievers. A church business meeting then becomes not "Thy will be done" but "my will be done." When Christ does not rule in the hearts of all the members, then it should be no surprise that carnality will abound.

But failing to discipline also has another consequence. It compromises the witness of the church. As I mentioned earlier, many unbelievers like to blame their unbelief on the fact that "All those church people are just a bunch of hypocrites. They're no different than anybody else." When churches refuse to discipline, those unbelievers are right. And the very people that we seek to persuade to be saved become unpersuadable because of the carnality of those who claim to be Christians. God commands his people to be holy just as he is holy (1 Pet 1:15-16).

Sinners ought to be able to get a glimpse of what God is like by looking at Christians. When a community fails to discipline, that holiness is compromised and so, therefore, is its witness. ∞

A WITNESSING COMMUNITY

Jim Stitzinger

Effective evangelism is measured not by individual responses, but by the clarity and accuracy of the message proclaimed. Whether in a large gathering or from one soul to another, a church functioning at maximum evangelistic capacity will saturate its areas of influence with the gospel of Jesus Christ. If your church ceased to exist, what evangelistic impact would be lost?

> Exhorting the church to evangelize should be as necessary as exhorting a newborn to cry; it should take effort to silence.

Evangelism should be instinctive to the church, a reflex that weaves its way in and through everything else it does together. Exhorting the church to evangelize should be as necessary as exhorting a newborn to cry; it should take effort to silence.

Far too often, the church functions as sheep in wolves clothing, hiding its identity and hoping to avoid detection. Scripture, however, knows nothing of an incognito Christian. Paul rather, calls believers ambassadors of Christ (2 Cor 5:20). An ambassador speaks the message they were given with the authority and conviction of the one who sends them.

As the church, the bride of Christ, our proclamation of the gospel must come with boldness. We look for points of intersection with the unbelieving world, not points of unification. As the church of Jesus Christ, our role is to carry the gospel so that salt and light collide with decay and darkness.

If the church is to function as the gospel witness to the nations, it must be vocal on an individual level. The church that is most effective in spreading the light of the gospel will be most active in the shadows, faithfully and boldly proclaiming the gospel to every unbeliever its members know. When believers are faithful to evangelize in the routine of life, they more naturally gather together in evangelistic efforts that flow beyond their immediate context and into the world.

The gauge of a church's evangelistic effectiveness is obedience on an individual level. The gospel commission is a call for individual disciples to engage individual sinners. The response of sinners is the work of the Spirit, not the result of our actions. Instead of gauging effectiveness by the response, gauge it by faithfulness to Christ's commission and accuracy of the message.

So, what are the hallmarks of a church functioning at

> Instead of gauging effectiveness by the response, gauge it by faithfulness to Christ's commission and accuracy with the message.

maximum evangelistic capacity? How can the church individually and collectively raise its evangelistic fervor? Here are a few encouragements for both church leaders and members. Though not exhaustive, they will hopefully help raise the voice for Christ-exalting, gospel-proclaiming evangelism in the local church.

1. Memorize the gospel

If you're saved, you know enough of the gospel to present it to someone else. However, it takes work to be clear and understandable. Every believer should commit to memory the basic components of the gospel. With those elements memorized, we should work daily to recite it to ourselves and even in role play with other believers. Seldom will you hold your Bible in hand when an evangelistic opportunity presents itself. While a memorized gospel presentation is not a prerequisite for evangelism, it will allow you to present the gospel with clarity and conviction.

If you're a pastor, set a goal for the entire church to commit the gospel to memory. No matter how young or advanced in years, every believer must have the gospel message spring-loaded, ready to give at any moment. A church that propagates is one that takes deliberate steps to keep the saving gospel message on the forefront of each believer's mind.

2. Recruit a prayer team

The hard work of evangelism begins on our knees, petitioning God to go before us in the hearts of those we engage with the gospel. No amount of human effort can save someone. So, in humility and dependency, we approach the throne of God with our prayers of intercession. This follows the pattern of Paul, who prays earnestly for his mission field when he says, "Brothers, my heart's desire and prayer to God for them is that they may be saved."

Not only does this step add

WHEN YOU PRAY, PRAY FOR

1. God to draw unbelievers to salvation. In John 6:44, Jesus says, "No one can come to me unless the Father who sent me draws him;"

2. The Spirit to accelerate the work of conviction. Jesus said, about the Spirit's ministry, that "when he comes, he will convict the world concerning sin and righteousness and judgment" (John 16:8);

3. God to reveal opportunities. We can follow Paul, who asked the Colossian church to "pray also for us, that God may open to us a door for the word, to declare the mystery of Christ" (Col 4:3); and

4. God to fill you with bold words. Again, Paul asked the Ephesian church to pray "also for me, that words may be given to me in opening my mouth boldly to proclaim the mystery of the gospel, for which I am an ambassador in chains, that I may declare it boldly, as I ought to speak" (Eph 6:19-20).

volume to our prayers as a church, it also creates accountability to keep one another in perpetual motion toward specific unbelievers. When we pray for specific unbelievers, as individuals and as groups, we grow increasingly aware of the opportunities Christ is giving to proclaim his name.

3. Live holy

The most clear and accurate gospel presentation is muted if unbelievers identify you by patterns of sin (anger, lust, gossip, laziness) instead of patterns of righteousness (love, joy, peace, patience, kindness, goodness, faithfulness, gentleness, self-control). In humility, repent when you sin, and use even your failures to magnify God's mercy. Let your holiness and repentance distinguish you from the world. The consistent example of a changed life is compelling proof of salvation.

4. Engage your personal mission field

As you read this today, who are the unbelievers you're engaging with the gospel? It's not enough to talk about them, you must talk with them, using the natural points of connection in your life to advance the gospel conversation. God, in his sovereign grace, chose

> God, in his sovereign grace, chose to place you in the context of those particular unbelievers. This is your mission field.

to place you in the context of those particular unbelievers. Don't throw away the opportunity to proclaim his saving message. This is your mission field.

You may find yourself in a season of life where you're insulated from the unbelieving world (living at a Christian college, at home with a believing family). Or, perhaps you have drifted toward the relationships of least resistance, surrounding yourself with like-minded Christians. If this is true for you, remember the example of Christ, who was always interacting with unbelievers (Luke 7:34; John 4:7-30), and then take the first step in the right direction.

Challenge yourself and other

believers to identify those to pursue with the gospel. At the same time, constantly work to create new networks that open up new mission fields for gospel ministry.

5. Relentlessly love other believers

The hard work of evangelism is carried out most vividly when believers speak and act with Christ-exalting love for one another. Jesus says, "A new commandment I give to you, that you love one another: just as I have loved you, you also are to love one another. By this all people will know that you are my disciples, if you have love for one another" (John 13:34-35).

Christian love is vital to evangelism because it makes the love of Christ visible for the world to see. The world is watching and must see the transforming power of the gospel on display

> Christian love is vital to evangelism because it makes the love of Christ visible for the world to see.

in our lives. This was at the heart of Paul's challenge to Philemon in extending forgiveness to Onesimus (Phlm 1:8-10).

The unbelieving world must see the Holy Spirit enabling Christians to serve one another, encourage one another, endure hardship, refuse gossip, speak the truth in love and embrace suffering. To what extent are the "one anothers" made visible in your relationships with other believers? Does your love for other believers give credibility to your gospel presentation?

6. Lead by example

No matter your age, level of responsibility or visibility within the church, you can lead by example. The heart of Paul's encouragement to Timothy is to lead by example despite his youth (1 Tim 4:12). Some of the greatest evangelists are those whose names we won't remember, but were relentlessly faithful to tell others about Jesus.

Those who lead by example in evangelism encourage others to fight the temptation to be lazy and complacent. Tell people about opportunities God has given you to share the gospel and encourage others to share their stories as well. Don't wait for someone else to lead by example, take initiative and others will follow.

7. Celebrate salvation

Never lose sight of the miracle that happens in new birth. If heaven explodes in celebration in response to the new birth, so should we. One way to do this is to share testimonies often. We can never hear enough of the work Christ has done in drawing someone to salvation. In your church, incorporate the recounting of salvation wherever possible. Doing so reminds us

The unbelieving world must see the Holy Spirit enabling Christians to serve one another, encourage one another, endure hardship, refuse gossip, speak the truth in love and embrace suffering.

> If heaven explodes in celebration in response to the new birth, so should we.

of the many ways the gospel penetrates hearts and how God chooses to use saved sinners in that process.

8. Maximize evangelistic gatherings

Certain church gatherings lend themselves to evangelistic purposes with greater clarity than others. For example, hold a Good Friday service in a local park or community center. In the weeks leading up to the evening, saturate the surrounding community with invitations, then maximize the service by presenting the gospel clearly. The same can be done with baptism. Hold a baptism service in a public setting and invite unbelieving family, friends and those you find along the way to listen to the testimonies of new believers.

Though many more could be added, these simple steps will develop a stronger evangelistic culture in your local church. Evangelism isn't just something we do, it's part of who we are. It's not a question of ability or adequacy, it's a question of obedience to Christ.

A church that loves Christ is a church that will not be stopped in its proclamation of the gospel and its demonstration of love for Christ. As ambassadors of Christ and the gospel, we can engage this world boldly and look forward to the work Christ will do in and through us, for his glory. ∞

—

FOR THE
CHRISTIAN

—

EVANGELISM
TO THE NEXT GENERATION

Troy W. Temple

"**W**hat's the greatest need for every young person in the world today?" That question has a ton of correct answers. Young people need help. They need healing. They need acceptance. They need safety. They need their parents. They need to be led. I could fill pages with answers that would overwhelm you and just might leave you believing that it's a hopeless venture. And you would be right.

The Need

After more than two decades of serving in youth ministry, I am overwhelmed more today than at any point in my brief history. The challenges that young people have faced in recent years have demonstrated that the enemy is more serious about the battle than the church. So let me answer the question: the greatest need for every young person in the world today is the need to know Jesus.

In Matthew 9:36, Jesus sees the crowd of people, "harassed and helpless" like sheep without a shepherd. That's what this generation of adolescents needs more than anything, a shepherd.

Jesus then exposes the real problem: a lack of laborers. His solution to the problem is for his people to "pray earnestly to the Lord of the harvest to send out laborers into his harvest." Reaching anyone with the gospel begins with God as we call out to him in prayer.

Better methods and more extensive research are not the way to introduce the next generation to the good shepherd. We've produced methods and research. The way to reach the next generation is for God to send people into the fields with a sense of urgency to reach them with the gospel.

Technology: A Symptom of a Deeper Issue

As I think about some of the current challenges facing young people – and the challenges they will face in the future – I can't help but think of technology. The next generation sees technology as the default mode for everything it does: music, money, relationships and recreation. They use it to connect with people, and they develop those relationships by exchanging the content of their lives. This has given way to habits that can become toxic.

Technology is not the issue, though. Instead, the way today's youth use technology points to a deeper, more foundational issue. It points to longings for relationships, relevance and meaning. These longings exist in every person in every generation, and this generation of youth has

> The greatest need for every young person in the world today is the need to know Jesus.

chosen technology as its voice, its language, its environment and the means of fulfilling these heart cries.

Authentic Relationships

This generation of youth sees through facades. When a person reaches about 12 years old, he or she develops a new part of anatomy, something I call a bologna detector. Whatever you call it, the next generation has an ability to detect a phony. Young people have been trained to do so from an early age because they've watched church-going adults say one thing and do a completely different thing. The next generation longs for people to be honest about the gospel and to live the message that they proclaim by demonstrating a genuine concern for them as people.

This kind of authenticity is so attractive to them because it's how Jesus lived. Jesus knew his message, and cared enough about people that he dined with sinners and tax collectors often (Matt 9:10). This generation of youth wants to see an authentic gospel lived out.

I grew up in Charlotte, N.C., where I was a member of a conservative, fundamentalist, Baptist church. There was no doubt that my church wanted to share the gospel with my city. The gospel message began with the redemptive story of the cross and the empty tomb, but it came with expectations that people change their lifestyle to fit into the church culture. In short, to be a Christian meant to show up at the church and look like a Christian, then avoid people who didn't look like you. But that's not even close to what the gospel is. The gospel isn't merely a set of "do's" and "don'ts" or a list of doctrines. The gospel is summed up in a person and what he did to rescue us. It revolves around an authentic relationship with Jesus Christ.

The church has focused on a gospel presentation when the next generation wants a gospel conversation. Too many Christians have allowed the gospel to be something they talk about once a week instead of something that has astonished them. People talk about what astonishes them. Tragically, what astonishes the next generation is how Christians can live their Christian lives in such mundane ways.

In Matthew 14, Jesus feeds more than 5,000 people with little more than a fast food meal, and then follows that up by walking on water. But the disciples show almost no signs of astonishment.

> As Christians, we've let the astonishing story of the gospel become a subtitle to a life marked by doing church things.

Then, Jesus gets into the boat and stops the storm. Finally, even the disciples can't miss what they've seen. Matthew records that "those in the boat worshipped him, saying, 'Truly you are the Son of God'" (Matt 14:33).

As Christians, we've let the astonishing story of the gospel become a subtitle to a life marked by doing church things. We need to recapture the ability to be astonished at Jesus and all he has done. The next generation needs to see us live our lives in true astonishment over the gospel. True joy in Christ is a compelling witness to the next generation.

If we truly desire to propagate the gospel to the next generation, there must be a new commitment to living an authentic gospel-centered life and to forging genuine relationships with the lost.

Relevant Application

I'm not sure where I first heard this, but it's true: nothing changes lives like seeing lives changed. The next generation is always interested in what really works; false claims are wasted on them. They've seen fantastic claims on infomercials for the last decade, and they've bought the products. What attracts them to such products is the personal testimony from people who have seen it work.

The next generation is hungry for a faith that "works," with relevant application to their lives. But we haven't taken the time to understand the issues that young people are struggling to overcome. Relevant application does not require that we find an answer for every felt need, it means that we are prepared to point the next generation to the truth found in God's Word. The Bible addresses their very real needs.

For example, the church can serve the next generation by showing them all that the Bible has to say about relationships, which are so important to them. We can show young people that relational conflict is caused by "passions at war within" them (Jas

4:1). Likewise, we can show them that healthy relationships result from service and sacrifice, and from a desire to "outdo one another in showing honor" (Rom 12:10).

These may be hard truths to hear, but the next generation will ultimately receive relevant truth that is not sugar-coated, but honest. In one instance, relationships have conflict because people are selfish. In the other instance, relationships are enriched when we serve one another. This is relevant truth that the next generation can apply every day, and it opens the door to introduce them to the good shepherd.

The next generation will continue to grapple with some of the most difficult issues our culture has ever seen, and they must know that the Bible speaks to all of those issues. We make a grave error when we attempt to explain the hard questions of life by saying "because the Bible says so." Instead, we should explain the way that God's Word is relevant to the lives of young people.

> The next generation will continue to grapple with some of the most difficult issues our culture has ever seen, and they must know that the Bible speaks to all of those issues.

Meaningful Purpose

During the past three decades, younger generations have increasingly migrated from pure consumeristic agendas to cause-oriented pursuits. Even the simplest decisions are measured by the possible impact on the immediate and global community. Life, for the next generation, must not only make sense; it must make a difference. The next generation is longing and intentionally searching for purpose.

As we share the message of the gospel with today's youth, they will continue to ask, "what difference does it make?" And they should. We all should. The gospel will always change the way we look at the world and respond to the brokenness that sin has inflicted on billions. So we can tell the next generation that the gospel commands our faithful attention toward those who hurt and need. Attending the needs of others is the meaningful purpose of the gospel. The activity of the gospel-centered life will carry out what Christ has instructed us to do.

Beginning with the words of Jesus in Matthew 25, we hear Jesus place a value on serving the hungry, the poor, the sick and the imprisoned in the body of Christ. When we attend to the needs of these brothers and sisters, we have served Jesus himself. The gospel expects that we care for the marginalized. Jesus told the young successful professional in Mark 10:21 to "go, sell all that you have and give to the poor," but he went away "sorrowful" because he loved his possessions. Jesus expected that his followers would find ways to care for the poor and sick.

This priority continues in James 1:27, where we read that, if our faith is ever to be clean and with a pure heart, then we are to care for the afflicted and remain untainted by the world. The meaningful purpose that this generation seeks is set to task by the gospel.

Matthew 22:37-40 presents a complete picture of meaningful purpose. Your primary purpose, if you're a Christian, is to "love the Lord with all your heart and with all your soul and with all your mind." If that is a true reality in our lives as Christ followers, then we will "love [our] neighbors as [ourselves]."

The gospel displays meaningful purpose most vividly in Christ's atoning sacrifice. The greatest purpose that the next generation could ever have is believing that message and loving their neighbors by sharing it with them. The next generation just needs to know that the gospel offers such a purpose.

Conclusion

Do you truly want to reach the next generation with the gospel? Live a life that is authentically gospel-centered. Then you will develop genuine relationships with those who need to meet the good shepherd. Lead them to the relevant truth of God's Word that meets the real needs that the next generation faces. Derive your meaningful purpose from the gospel, demonstrating the same value for others that Jesus did.

The next generation is poised to receive the good news. ∞

EVANGELISM
TO NOMINAL CHRISTIANS

Owen Strachan

Disruption is not fun.

You know the scene: you're working, trying your best to plug into a task, whether a paper, a sermon or a document for work, and your phone buzzes. Or your email inbox signals the arrival of a new message. Or your friend stops by, and you're glad to see him, but he doesn't realize that your leg is uncontrollably tapping not because you're invested in the conversation, but because you have 13 tasks to do in the next two hours.

But there's another kind of disruption that's good for us. The term "disruption" comes from the business world. Professor Clayton Christensen of Harvard Business School has popularized the term "disruptive innovation" or "creative disruption," as it's often called. He claims business leaders need to see what areas of their company need shaking up. Corporations and the people who work in them can fall into patterns of ease and complacency. Christensen advocates that leaders regularly "disrupt" the business by trimming what is unnecessary and sharpening what is profitable.

The church is not a business. It's a living, breathing, spiritual organism, the body of Christ. But here's the thing: I think the

> The church is not a business. It's a living, breathing, spiritual organism, the body of Christ.

practice of "creative disruption" predates Christensen's insight. It seems like a new concept, but it's actually an old one.

Two thousand years old, in fact.

And it comes not from the marketplace of commerce, but the mind of Christ.

Jesus Gets Disruptive

In Matthew 13:1-9, Jesus tells a startling story, the parable of the soils. This is no disquisition on conservation of the earth, however. It's a spiritual shakeup, one announcing that not all who seem to have faith will, in the end, be saved:

> That same day Jesus went out of the house and sat beside the sea. And great crowds gathered about him, so that he got into a boat and sat down. And the whole crowd stood on the beach. And he told them many things in parables, saying: "A sower went out to sow. And as he sowed, some seeds fell along the path, and the birds came and devoured them. Other seeds fell on rocky ground, where they did not have much soil, and immediately they sprang up, since they had no depth of soil, but when the sun rose they were scorched. And since they had no root, they

withered away. Other seeds fell among thorns, and the thorns grew up and choked them. Other seeds fell on good soil and produced grain, some a hundredfold, some sixty, some thirty. He who has ears, let him hear."

Just a few verses later, Jesus delivers a second, equally stunning parable. In Matthew 13:24-30, Christ tells the parable of the wheat and the tares:

He [Jesus] put another parable before them, saying, "The kingdom of heaven may be compared to a man who sowed good seed in his field, but while his men were sleeping, his enemy came and sowed weeds among the wheat and went away. So when the plants came up and bore grain, then the weeds appeared also. And the servants of the master of the house came and said to him, 'Master, did you not sow good seed in your field? How then does it have weeds?' He said to them, 'An enemy has done this.' So the servants said to him, 'Then do you want us to go and gather them?' But he said, 'No, lest in gathering the weeds you root up the wheat along with them. Let both grow together until the harvest, and at harvest time I will tell the reapers, Gather the weeds first and bind them in bundles to be burned, but gather the wheat into my barn.'"

There is much to unpack in each of these parables. For our purposes, we note a common thread between the two, that not all who seem to be Christians are in fact saved. In the first parable, three out of the four examples of "seed" show themselves, ultimately, to be unbelievers. The birds almost immediately devour the first kind of seed; the sun scorches the second kind after an initial burst; the thorns choke the third kind after a period. Christ's examples show us that as we preach the gospel, we will encounter people who initially profess faith but who ultimately show themselves to be unconverted.

Jesus underscores this same idea in the second parable. The weeds and wheat grow together for a long while. At the end of life, it becomes apparent that some people who consider themselves "wheat" – true believers – are in fact unbelievers. They never truly repented of their sin and believed in Jesus Christ as their Savior. It is these people who will be cast

Nominal Christianity develops when the gospel is dumbed down and made "uncostly."

away from the presence of Christ and banished to eternal darkness when he returns.

In both parables, we encounter a problem we're aware of but may not be able to name: "nominal" Christianity, or Christianity in name only (not reality). This develops when the gospel is dumbed down and made "uncostly," when the church does not call for a transformed life as evidence of salvation and when congregations do not practice church discipline to guard the gospel. If this sounds like a foreboding but far-off problem, it's not.

It's as near as your local church.

Nominal Christianity became a particular challenge in the twentieth century. Many evangelical churches believed that they needed to embrace business practices in congregational life in order to draw new members. They shifted into a model of church in which congregants were treated as consumers, with the church itself providing them the services or experiences they wanted. In some cases, these assemblies did not emphasize a transformed life as a necessary mark of ongoing membership. It was enough to make an initial profession of faith; church discipline was largely lost as a means of promoting the gospel.

These trends resulted in churches with far more people on the rolls than actually belonged. Beyond this, many people came to think of themselves as saved who showed little or no spiritual fruit (Matt 9:27). Because of this, nominal Christianity became a troublesome part – a sizeable part – of many local churches.

This problem persists in our day.

Disrupting the Comforted

What is the secret to solving this widespread challenge to true Christianity? Well, there's no magic bullet. Pastors and concerned members need to pray to the Lord. They need to ask him to send revival to their churches in order that people who have deceived themselves might be won to Christ.

God's grace alone can solve this problem.

This does not mean, however, that pastors are helpless. God's grace is always an empowering grace, as texts like Romans 6:6 show us. Sin has been crucified with Christ, and we possess all we need for life and godliness, as 2 Peter 1:3 makes clear. What should gospel-loving Christians do, then, to address nominal Christianity, and to show love to those who profess faith but do not evidence it?

In answering this, the concept of "creative disruption" comes into play. Actually, for our purposes, we need "Christic disruption," or "gospel disruption." What does this mean?

It means that pastors cannot

> Pastors cannot speak soft words to hard-hearted people, those who sit in our pews each week but resist the transformation of the gospel.

speak soft words to hard-hearted people, those who sit in our pews each week but resist the transformation of the gospel. We cannot abide faith in name only. We cannot content ourselves with a thirty-minute message, a few songs and a handshake at the door. Instead, as pastors and church leaders, we see ourselves as disruptors of a sleeping church.

We are not cruel in this regard; we're not hearkening back to summer camp as a kid, pulling pranks on sleeping friends. No, out of love for people who are in eternal jeopardy, we preach the gospel as a summons to repentant faith.

As with John to the church in Sardis, we boldly say this:

> Wake up, and strengthen what remains and is about to die, for I have not found your works complete in the sight of my God. Remember, then, what you received and heard. Keep it, and repent. If you will not wake up, I will come like a thief, and you will not know at what hour I will come against you (Rev 3:2-3).

How can we appropriately mimic John in calling professing believers to robust faith? Here are some practical ways we can carry out this duty of love:

1. Preach true Christianity from the pulpit. Identify the marks of grace and the fruit of the Spirit (Gal 5:22-23);

2. Call people to embrace true Christianity. Make clear that the duty to repent and believe is an immanent one – we are not to put off faith and repentance;

3. Make clear that grace is not "cheap," but "costly," as Dietrich Bonhoeffer famously said. True faith, in other words, does not ask, "What is the minimum I can do to be saved?" Rather, it confesses "You have the words of life" to Christ, necessitating that we reject the world and embrace the Messiah (John 6:68);

4. Love your people. If you only call them to faith, but do not make a serious effort to care for them and demonstrate that you have the utmost care for their souls, expect that they will tune you out. On the other hand, you may well see the Lord soften their hearts through a persistent, kind, gospel-saturated witness;

5. Lead well and boldly. Show by courageous, convictional leadership that you will not be swayed by opposition, which you should expect if you challenge Satan on turf he's claimed;

6. Surprise those you think may be nominal Christians by repenting when you're wrong. Many people have rarely seen genuine and full-throated contrition over sin. Seeing it afresh – or for the first time – will speak a stronger word than you might think;

7. Don't assume that you know the hearts of fellow sinners as God does. Gather as much data as you can, pray for discernment, but be careful to conclude, and to say, that someone is for certain not a Christian;

8. Pray for God to work among your people. Remember Psalm 127:1, which reads, "Unless the Lord builds the house, those who build it labor in vain;"

9. Constantly keep in mind that you cannot rescue nominal Christians, but the Lord can; and

10. Practice church discipline according to texts like Matthew 18:15-20 and 1 Corinthians 5-6, knowing as you do so that just as gospel preaching promotes Christ, so does guarding the gospel through

the preservation of a healthy church that shows the world the reality of spiritual transformation (though not perfection).

Conclusion

The problem of nominalism is far more difficult in nature than are the daily interruptions to our workflow. This is an ancient quagmire, as Christ's own parables shows. It is not a challenge faced only by unfaithful or subpar pastors and churches. It is a burden that every shepherd and every assembly will bear at some point and in some fashion.

This was true of America's best-known shepherd, the pastor-theologian Jonathan Edwards. Edwards was a peerless preacher, yet he struggled almost continually with professing believers who would not wholeheartedly commit to the work of God. This was due in part to the fact that many people had joined the church as members from infancy yet had never fully owned the faith. For this reason, Edwards constantly exercised a ministry of gospel disruption, an effort that led both to the fires of revival and to his own firing. Some embraced his call to repentance; others steeled their hearts against it and fought him.

We must remember examples like this. We must also call to mind Edwards's world-shaking preaching, with its focus on the perils of sin (as seen in the famous sermon, "Sinners in the Hands of an Angry God") and the glories of true and saving faith. As we pursue our own ministries of capitalize disruption, let's hold out what Edwards calls the "true sense" of the things of God, knowing as we do that only he can make fellow sinners taste it. As he put it in his majestic sermon, "A Divine and Supernatural Light," saving faith is driven by

> A true sense of the divine and superlative excellency of the things of religion; a real sense of the excellency of God, and Jesus Christ, and of the work of redemption, and the ways

> Nominalism is a burden that every shepherd and every assembly will bear at some point and in some fashion.

and works of God revealed in the gospel. There is a divine and superlative glory in these things; an excellency that is of a vastly higher kind, and more sublime nature, than in other things; a glory greatly distinguishing them from all that is earthly and temporal. He that is spiritually enlightened truly apprehends and sees it, or has a sense of it. He doesn't merely rationally believe that God is glorious, but he has a sense of the gloriousness of God in his heart. There is not only a rational belief that God is holy, and that holiness is a good thing; but there is a sense of the loveliness of God's holiness. There is not only a speculatively judging that God is gracious, but a sense how amiable God is upon that account; or a sense of the beauty of this divine attribute.

May we sense this beauty afresh today, and propagate it in our churches for the salvation of souls and the glory of almighty God. ∞

RESOURCES

Mike McKinley, *Am I Really a Christian?* (Crossway/9Marks, 2011).

Owen Strachan and Douglas Sweeney, *Jonathan Edwards on True Christianity* (part of the five-volume *Essential Edwards Collection*, Moody, 2010).

Mark Dever, *The Church: The Gospel Made Visible* (Lifeway, 2012).

John Piper, *Finally Alive* (Christian Focus, 2009).

EVANGELISM
TO WORLD RELIGIONS

Travis Kerns

Imagine the following situation. You're talking to a group of people in a coffee shop, and the issue of religion comes up. Having just met them, you don't know the religious beliefs of the others around you, so you bring up the teachings of Jesus. You make the claim that the teachings of Jesus are worthy of consideration and tell those gathered around the table that Jesus has changed your life, both now and forever. Someone at the table asks why Jesus is so important, so you tell him that Jesus claimed to be God's Son.

You go on to explain that only through faith in Jesus can a person's sins be forgiven and, immediately, the conversation gets heated. One person exclaims, "I'm not a sinner." Another says, "You're not God. You can't tell me how to live." A third person responds, "Just because a person doesn't know Jesus doesn't make him bad. There are good people in other religions. They don't need Jesus; they've got their own way to God. Don't be so one-sided and intolerant. Leave them alone." Their reactions surprise you

Accusations of intolerance, unfairness and bigotry are common whenever Christians talk about Jesus as the only way to God.

and leave you helpless, hopeless and drained.

Accusations of intolerance, unfairness and bigotry – and the thought processes leading to those proclamations – are common whenever Christians talk about Jesus as the only way to God. Christians often don't know how to respond to such accusations, and may even wonder if the objectors, like those in the conversation above, are right. Maybe people in other religions really are okay. Maybe they really don't need Jesus. Maybe God has provided a way for members of other religions to be saved. After all, it's not fair that a person needs to hear about and know Jesus just to get into heaven, right?

In order to think through these issues rightly, we must answer three specific questions. First, why should Christians be concerned about spreading the teachings of Jesus, especially to persons involved in other religions? Second, what is the message of Christianity? Third, how should we present the teachings of Christianity to non-Christians? Lord willing, the discussion that follows will help you understand why there is a need, what the message of Christianity is, and how to present that message in the most effective way possible.

Why Be Concerned?

Why should Christians be concerned about spreading the teachings of Jesus, especially to persons involved in other religions? This is an important question for all Christians to answer, and a few New Testament passages will help answer it.

The first passage is 1 Peter 3:14-15. In this passage, Peter writes:

> But even if you should suffer for righteousness' sake, you will be blessed. Have no fear of them, nor be troubled, but in your hearts honor Christ the Lord as holy, always being prepared to make a defense to anyone who asks you for a reason for the hope that is in you; yet do it with gentleness and respect.

Peter notes that obedient Christians will likely face suffering, and such suffering should be received as a blessing, because the believer has the honor to suffer for the sake of Christ.

Verse 15 is most instructive for our purposes. Peter writes that we should honor Christ, or set him apart, as Lord in our hearts. The way to honor Christ is to be prepared to talk about Christ at any moment. Anytime a non-

Jesus is not just one way among many, he is the only way.

Christian asks a Christian why he is so happy, joyful and hopeful, the Christian is to be ready with a response. Also important is the manner in which Peter instructs Christians to answer non-Christians: with gentleness and respect. Christians are not only to talk about the mercy and grace of God in Christ, but also to show the mercy and grace of God in Christ with our actions and words. When non-Christians ask us to defend our hope, we are commanded by Scripture to give an answer, and we honor Christ when we do so. We'll discuss what that answer should be later.

The second passage is John 14:6. John records the words of Jesus: "I am the way, and the truth, and the life; no one comes to the Father except through me." This verse is crucial for the non-Christian, especially for the member of another religion. Put simply, Jesus declares that the only way to God the Father is himself, Jesus the Son. Notice Jesus does not say he is a way, a truth or a life, but he says he is the way, the truth and the life. Here, Jesus tells his listeners – and us as readers – that he is the only way to get to God. Jesus is not just one way among many, he is the only way. Indeed, Jesus is the only road leading to God the Father.

The third passage is Acts 4:12, where Luke records Peter's sermon after Peter and John are arrested for spreading the gospel. Concerning Jesus, Peter declares that "There is salvation in no one else; for there is no other name under heaven given among men by which we must be saved." Peter affirms that, similar to John 14:6, Jesus is undeniably the only way to find salvation. Salvation is not found in the teachings of any other religious figure or religious leader; salvation is found only in and through Jesus.

So, Christians should be concerned with the spread of Christ's message to members of other religions because (1) it is a means of honoring Christ, (2) other religions do not follow Jesus and (3) though members of other religions think they have found salvation, they have not found anything.

What's the Message of Christianity?

Now that we understand why we should be concerned for members of other religions, we come to our second question: what is the message of Christianity? The message of Christianity is a profoundly simple message of sin, atonement and redemption, all through Christ. If the message is so simple (though not simplistic), is there an easy way to share the message? In this section, let's consider an easy way to share the message of Jesus, a way known commonly as the Romans Road.

The Romans Road is a simple way to share the gospel with non-Christians, consisting of six passages:

1. Romans 3:23, everyone has sinned and fallen short of God's perfect standard, his glory.

> Salvation is not found in the teachings of any other religious figure or leader; salvation is found only in and through Jesus.

2. Romans 6:23, there is a penalty for sin: physical and spiritual death, and which also makes the free offer of eternal life from God through Jesus Christ.

3. Romans 5:8, Jesus has died for sinners.

4. Romans 10:9-10, salvation is offered through confession of Jesus and real belief that God raised Jesus from the dead.

5. Romans 5:1, true, lasting peace with God the Father is offered only through justification by faith. In other words, humans can have peace with God even though they are all sinners and have all fallen short of his perfect standard. The only way to have peace is through trusting Christ and believing in his work and message.

6. Romans 8:1, eternal condemnation for sin is now no longer a worry for the person who trusts in Christ.

Thus, the message of Christianity is simple. All humans are sinners; all have missed God's perfect, required standard. All humans receive physical and spiritual death as payment for their sin. However, God has provided a way to escape the spiritual death we

The only way to find true and lasting peace with God is by confessing Jesus as Lord.

so rightly deserve, and the way of escape is the free gift of eternal life offered by God the Father through Jesus Christ the Son, who died for sinners. Only by confessing Jesus as Lord and believing in him can anyone escape spiritual death. Likewise, the only way to find true and lasting peace with God is by confessing Jesus as Lord and believing in him. After doing so, the new Christian finds no more need to be concerned about eternal condemnation.

How Should Christians Talk to Members of World Religions?

Unfortunately, Christians occasionally treat members of other religions of the world as inferior to them, and may even take the opportunity to be a "jerk for Jesus." This is not only unfortunate, but unbiblical. As we saw in 1 Peter 3:15 earlier, the Holy Spirit, through Peter's pen, commands followers of Jesus to be gentle and respectful when interacting with unbelievers about the gospel. Telling the non-Christian the gospel is confrontational in itself; the Christian need not make it more so. When the non-Christian hears that he is a sinner, that he deserves physical and spiritual death and that the only way to escape is by placing his faith and trust in Jesus, the non-believer will be offended by the message. There is no reason for the Christian to add more offense to the message by his conduct.

How, then, should Christians interact with members of other religions? Is there a good, practical guide for doing evangelism?

> Telling the non-Christian the gospel is confrontational in itself; the Christian need not make it more so.

Former dean of Harvard Divinity School, Krister Stendahl, when he spoke to a gathered media press conference in 1985, gave three basic rules for interacting with members of other religious groups, and his three "rules of religious understanding" can be very instructive for our purposes.

Stendahl's first rule is that Christians should learn about the beliefs of another religion from members of that religion. We would expect this from others as well. Any time Christianity is the subject of a news report or something of that nature, Christians are usually interviewed for their view. In the same way, if Buddhism is the subject of a news report or media feature, Buddhists are usually interviewed about their Buddhism. This is a normal occurrence within our culture, and our evangelism should focus on the beliefs of others in the same way. If your calling in life is to minister to Muslims and you would like to know what Muslims believe, ask a Muslim. If your calling in life is to minister to Mormons and you would like to know what Mormons believe, ask a Mormon. This is not to say there is no place for books, articles or explanations about religions by non-members. There is absolutely a place, a much needed place, for works of that sort. Comparative religion is a vitally important field and more work needs to be done in that area. This first rule is simply that the most accurate understanding of a particular religion and its belief system is likely to come from a member of that religion.

Stendahl's second rule is that we should make fair comparisons. When listening to debates between members of various religions or reading works by members of various religions, make sure to listen to debates between parallel speakers or to read works by parallel writers. By this, Stendahl simply means that we should compare apples to apples and oranges to oranges. Don't read a work about Jesus by a Christian with a Ph.D. and compare it to a work about Jesus by a Muslim layman. Don't read a work about creation by a Buddhist with a Ph.D. and compare it to a work about creation by a Hindu layman. Likewise, don't compare the Christianity of David Koresh or Jim Jones to the Hinduism of Mahatma Gandhi, and don't compare the Islam of terrorists to the Christianity of Mother Teresa. Put simply, compare equals and you'll be on the right path toward understanding for the sake of evangelism.

Stendahl's third rule is that we should leave room for "holy envy." Though this sounds a bit ecumenical, Stendahl simply means there are likely aspects of other religions, and aspects of the lives of members of other religions, from which we can learn. Here, the Christian does not need to agree with the other religion or with the member of the other religion, but he can recognize that the Buddhist may pray more intently, the Hindu may believe more strongly, the

If the Christian believes he is absolutely, objectively correct in his belief, he should have the most intense prayer, the strongest belief, the most liberal giving and the fullest love.

Mormon may give more liberally or the Jew may love more fully than the Christian. This is where holy envy is found. If the Christian believes he is absolutely, objectively correct in his belief, he should have the most intense prayer, the strongest belief, the most liberal giving and the fullest love. The devotion of members of other religions should drive Christians to be even more serious about their deeply held convictions.

Conclusion

Our final question, then, is somewhat borrowed from Francis Schaeffer: namely, how should we then evangelize? How can we most effectively propagate the gospel to world religions? First, we pray. 1 Thessalonians 5:17 commands us to pray continually, and our prayers should include petitions for opportunity to speak with members of other religions, boldness when confronting false belief and compassion over the lost condition of those involved in other religions.

Second, we study. 1 Peter 3:15 commands us to be ready to give a defense for our hope in Christ whenever we are asked. The best way to defend the hope we have is to know what others believe and to be ready to ask them difficult questions as we present Christ to them. Acts 17 serves as a good example of how the early church did this very thing.

Third, we go. Matthew 28:18-20 commands us to go into all the world, proclaiming the gospel and making disciples.

May God grant us the courage, the boldness, the compassion, the ability and the burden to propagate the gospel to members of the world's religions. ∞

EVANGELISM
TO MUSLIMS

John Klaassen

Every Wednesday a Muslim woman would come to meet with a group of ladies at our house. Over sweet mint tea, they would start in the Old Testament and work their way toward Jesus. After they met, the woman would leave as quickly as she came. Then, one day, it all changed. Jesus became more than a prophet to her, more than a name in history. On that day, Jesus became God incarnate, Savior and

Lord. Not long after, she followed her Savior in baptism with her new sisters in Christ, confessing a new birth and a new life.

Sharing the gospel with Muslims is one of the great privileges I have had in my lifetime. Some of my greatest memories are of sitting on the floor, telling people Old Testament stories of sacrifice and service to God, and then talking about what it means for Jesus to be God and the ultimate sacrifice.

One day, a friend with whom we had shared the gospel many times said to me, "John, I think you are right, Jesus did suffer on the cross for my sins." For a Muslim, this was a big step. But not big enough, so we kept telling him biblical stories of faith and Jesus. Sometime later he said, "John, I think you are right, Jesus did die on the cross for my sins." Then he added, "And Jesus and the Prophet, they are the same." Again a big step, but not enough, so we kept telling him biblical stories and sharing how Jesus is much more than any prophet that ever lived. Finally, one day, he said "You are right, Jesus is God, he is Savior, he is Lord." On that day, he took a step of faith, "confessing with his mouth Jesus as Lord" (Rom 10:9-10).

When most of us think of

When most of us think of Islam and Muslims, we think of extremists and terrorists. Instead, we should think of our Muslim neighbors down the street.

Islam and Muslims, we think of extremists and terrorists. Our images are of women wearing burkas and men in head scarves. Instead, we should think of our Muslim neighbors down the street, worried about their kid's education, how things are going at work and about their marriages and in-laws. They're not so different from you and me. So how do you share your faith with a Muslim? When I think of sharing my faith with a Muslim, I like to think in terms of C. Peter Wagner's 3 P's in evangelism: presence, proclamation and persuasion. I like to add a fourth "P:" prayer, which is the foundation of all of our evangelism. Think of these four P's as building blocks forming a pyramid.

Prayer

Prayer is the biggest block and the foundation for working with any people group. To neglect this block is to take away your foundation and ignore what God wants to do in the lives of the people with whom you work. Jesus says in Luke 10, "The harvest is plentiful, but the laborers are few. Therefore pray earnestly to the Lord of the harvest to send out laborers into his harvest."

Jesus reminds his hearers that there is a harvest. In the time I have worked with Muslims – more than 22 years now – I have been reminded over and over again that the Lord is calling out his own from among the most forgotten people groups all over the world, including people from the hardest Islamic sects and restricted access nations. It's noteworthy that Jesus does not ask us to pray for people in need of the gospel. Rather, he directs us to pray for more workers.

God is working in Muslim lives. We pray that God will call and send thousands more into the harvest fields of Islamic lands and even places like the U.S. and Europe, where refugees from countries where we have little to no access are coming to us. If God has placed a Muslim in your life, you have a responsibility to share the gospel with him. You are an answer to the prayer for laborers.

It's important to understand that prayer, as one of the five pillars of Islam, is also important to the Muslim. If a Muslim practices these five pillars – confession, daily prayers, almsgiving, Ramadan and the pilgrimage to Mecca – perfectly, he could possibly earn his way to heaven. Muslims recite a ritual prayer five times a day, facing Mecca. This prayer is called the "salah." Many believe that is the extent of their prayers, but Muslims also pray throughout their day with supplications known as the "dua." When praying the "dua," Muslims hold their hands open in front

When you pray with a Muslim, though, always close your prayer with "in the name of Jesus."

of the chest, raise their eyes to heaven and make petition and praise to Allah. These prayers are offered anytime, anywhere.

Often, after eating in our Muslim friends' homes, our friends would offer the "dua." When we had Muslim friends in our home, we would do the same. Praying with a Muslim (offering the "dua," not the "salah") is one of the great acts you can perform with your Muslim friend. Offering to pray for them and to pray with them distinguishes you from other westerners and helps them understand that you're a person of prayer who knows God.

When you pray with a Muslim, though, always close your prayer with "in the name of Jesus." When you pray in the name of Jesus (John 14:13-14), you pray with power, and you pray in a way that is distinctly Christian.

Presence

Presence, the second largest of our blocks, is about being with your Muslim friends. Muslims, and middle-easterners in general, are event-oriented people. It's not about "quality time" for them; it's about the quantity of time you spend with them. This is difficult for most of us to understand because we lead busy lives that leave little time for friendship.

> If you plan to share the gospel with your Muslim friends, you need to carve time out of your schedule to be with them.

However, if you plan to share the gospel with your Muslim friends, you need to carve time out of your schedule to be with them. Invite them to go places with you, even if it seems mundane. Remember, it's about time, do not worry about what you are doing; just be with them.

As you spend time with your Muslim friends, it's important that you help them with the needs they have here in the U.S. When you go to their home, ask if you can help them with something. Maybe they need help with a letter they received from their school about their kids, but they do not understand what they are supposed to do. Perhaps they need help making a doctor's visit or going to the dentist.

If they're immigrants to the

U.S., take them grocery shopping and show them the things you buy. Something as simple as navigating the grocery store can make a difference; in their home country there are probably only one or two choices for something like milk or bread. In the U.S., the options may overwhelm them. When my wife and I lived overseas, it was incredible to find those friends who helped us understand how schools and doctors worked. So do likewise, help your Muslim friend figure out those differences, and you will win a friend for life.

If you live overseas, make sure the native people understand your role in the community and how you add value to it. If you run a business, make a profit and work at your business. While overseas, we worked for a humanitarian relief agency. The neighbors saw me go to work every day and saw the results of our aid and development work. At times, they asked us to visit other villages to do development work there. The key is to make sure your job is legitimate and that you produce something of value. If you do not assign yourself a "role" they understand, then the community will assign you a role, and it might not be the "role" for which you had hoped.

Proclamation

Proclamation is sharing of the good news, and the pyramid cannot exist without it. Religious conversations are never difficult to get into with a Muslim, but they can be difficult to end without starting a debate. If you have practiced the first two "P's," you'll find that your friend will listen to you. But don't wait to start proclaiming the good news of Jesus. From the very beginning, establish the fact that you are a follower of Jesus, and that he makes a difference in your life. Talk to them about your prayer life and what God is doing in your life.

One way to initiate a good conversation is to ask your friend if you can share your story with them about how God has changed your life, and then share your testimony with your friend. Remember, though, everyone has a story. You might find that your Muslim friend has a similar story to yours about how Islam has changed his life, so don't just stop with your story, but share a biblical story as well. When I share my testimony I also tell the story of Cornelius in Acts 10, emphasizing that Cornelius was a godly man by everyone's standards, but that was not enough. He still needed Jesus in his life, so God sent Peter to tell him the rest of the story. I then tell my friend that I am there to tell him the rest of the story.

From that point, you can share the gospel story of God's redeeming act from creation to the cross. Remember to emphasize that God created us to have a relationship with him, but sin has destroyed that relationship (Gen 1-3). Only the blood of sacrifice can bring about the forgiveness of sins (Heb 9:22), and God provided Jesus as the ultimate sacrifice, the propitiation for our sins (Rom 3:25; Heb 2:17). In other words, as the perfect sacrifice, Jesus took on the wrath of God for our sins.

The first time you share this story, your Muslim friend will argue that God would never have allowed Jesus to die on the cross. Don't worry, just keep telling the story and reminding him of the importance of sacrifice. It will take time and multiple tellings of the same story, but God will slowly work on his heart and begin to awaken your friend to the truth of the gospel.

Persuasion

The smallest of the "P's" is persuasion, which is also the point of the pyramid – or the tip of the spear, to use another metaphor. Once you've established

> Never, ever deny the truth of the gospel, no matter what the situation.

a strong relationship with your friend, you can say what needs to be said. You must eventually share that Jesus is the only way to have peace with God. You must share that, without repentance, there is no forgiveness for sins. You must share that Jesus is God.

When your friend argues with you, don't back down. Respond with affection in your voice. If he offends you, you can articulate that, but continue to pursue him with love. And never, ever deny the truth of the gospel, no matter what the situation.

It's in persuasion that contextualization is most powerful, but remember that contextualization never softens the gospel; it clarifies the gospel in such a way that the truth penetrates the heart of the hearer so that he can no longer ignore the truth of the gospel, but must act on what he has heard. Acceptance or rejection of the gospel is no longer dependent on you, but on God.

A Bridge

Finally, let me give you an easy-to-remember bridge to use as you share the gospel with your Muslim friend. Whenever you meet Muslims, they'll say, "As-salam alaykum," meaning "peace be on you." Ask them about that peace, where it comes from, how it's attained, whether anyone can have it and why there is such a lack of peace on earth. Then ask if you can tell them a story.

Share with them the creation story. The Genesis account is rich – not too different from their own account – and will provide a common ground. After God created everything, he said it was good. All of creation was at peace with God; all of creation was at peace with itself. In fact, Moses tells us in Genesis 2:25 that the man and woman were naked and not ashamed. Everything was perfect – there was no fear, and there was no shame in the garden.

Then, sin entered through the disobedience of Adam and Eve. The first thing Adam and Eve did after their sin was to make coverings for themselves. For the first time in their lives they knew shame and fear. When God came to walk with them in the cool of the garden, they hid. For the first time in history, peace was broken between God and man, mankind with itself and man and nature.

The curse that God placed on nature, mankind and the serpent was a result of one sin. The curse can be summed up as the elimination of peace on earth. Since Adam, we have lived in enmity with God, others and nature. Because of our sin, there is nothing we can do to restore our relationship with God. Our sin broke the relationship with God and only he can restore it. Jesus came to restore that relationship, to pay the penalty for our sins and to create a path to God by dying and rising from the dead.

Remember, your Muslim friend probably won't embrace the whole story the first time you tell it. Sharing your faith with a Muslim is about prayer, presence, proclamation and persuasion. There are no shortcuts. It doesn't typically happen overnight, but as your friend listens to the truth of the gospel, God's Spirit will work. John writes in Revelation 7:9-10,

> After this I looked, and behold, a great multitude that no one could number, from every nation, from all tribes and peoples and languages, standing before the throne and before the Lamb, clothed in white robes, with palm branches in their

> One day in heaven, there will be a multitude so large that no one can count it. Your friend, who seems so hard right now, may be one of them.

hands, and crying out with a loud voice, "Salvation belongs to our God who sits on the throne, and to the Lamb!" And all the angels were standing around the throne and around the elders and the four living creatures, and they fell on their faces before the throne and worshiped God, saying, "Amen! Blessing and glory and wisdom and thanksgiving and honor and power and might be to our God forever and ever! Amen."

One day in heaven, there will be a multitude so large that no one can count it. In that number will be men and women from every place on earth. Brothers and sisters from the hardest places on earth will stand before the throne. Your friend, who seems so hard right now, may be one of them.

We see also that salvation is attributed to God, and also "to the lamb." Your Muslim friend will never get to heaven apart from the lamb. For that matter, no one gets to heaven apart from the lamb. John quotes Jesus as saying, "I am the way, and the truth, and the life. No one comes to the Father except through me" (John 14:6). Paul reminds us in Romans, "How then will they call on him in whom they have not believed? And how are they to believe in him of whom they have never heard? And how are they to hear without someone preaching?" (Rom 10:14)

No Jesus means no salvation, no hope and no peace with God. Will you be the one to take the gospel to your Muslim neighbor, friend or coworker? If not you, then who will get that privilege? Do not miss out; share your faith with a Muslim. ∞

EVANGELISM
TO SKEPTICS

Dan DeWitt

Sharing the gospel with skeptics is not an endeavor to be taken lightly. It is a risky enterprise, and the greatest risks involve the apologist's own soul. That's why C.S. Lewis, in the midst of his WWII evangelistic endeavors, warned youth leaders of the need to walk circumspectly when operating on the front lines of apologetic activity:

That is why we apologists take our lives in our hands and can be saved only by falling back continually from the web of our own arguments, as from our intellectual counters, into the Reality — from Christian apologetics into Christ Himself. That also is why we need one another's continual help.

In addition to risking public reputation, and the real possibility of spiritual fatigue, the apologist will also be forced to come face-to-face with his true convictions. The apologist's views will be laughed at, and his commitments scorned. Unless the evangelist to skeptics is adequately rooted and established in his convictions, there will be temptation to dilute beliefs in order to earn credibility.

A great deal of these temptations stem from a lack of confidence in the gospel and a misunderstanding of the nature of ministry to skeptics. Many think evangelism aimed at this demographic is limited to apologetics, a defense of the faith. This notion is too narrow, though. Evangelism is not merely negative and reactive.

Seeing evangelism as negative and reactive can lead to a passive witness instead of an intentional and positive assertion of the truth. That's why evangelism in any setting should include both an affirmation of what the gospel is as well as a defense against objections and misunderstandings. Without a balanced approach, the apologist will be tempted to abdicate certain biblical foundations for the sake of establishing neutral ground.

So what is the best way to share the gospel with skeptics? What is the best form of apologetics? Those familiar with the nuances of apologetic approaches will know that there is no shortage

Unless the evangelist to skeptics is adequately rooted and established in his convictions, there will be temptation to dilute beliefs in order to earn credibility.

of controversy regarding which form is the most biblical, so I don't intend to answer these questions for you in this brief chapter. Instead, I'd suggest that you consider a book like Steve Cowan's *Five Views on Apologetics* to inform, shape and refine your own convictions. What I would like to offer are seven imperatives, or broad categories, for sharing the gospel with skeptics. These are parameters to keep your gospel witness on track without falling into compromise.

Regardless of the strategy you use, the following principles will allow you to do evangelistic work among skeptics for the advancement of the kingdom and the glory of God.

Seven Imperatives for Sharing the Gospel with Skeptics

1. PRESENT TRUTH AS KNOWABLE

Christians can easily become intimidated when sharing the gospel with the "intelligentsia." This should not be so. The believer need not assume a position of weakness when talking with skeptics. The Christian worldview offers much more than many people realize when it comes to describing reality. In fact, an atheistic worldview is actually forced to borrow certain assumptions that flow from a theistic outlook in order to formulate an argument against it.

Consider how we use the basic laws of logic in our everyday conversations. The law of non-contradiction, for example, is utilized in evaluating truth claims. This is the principle that something cannot be both true and false at the same time and in the same way. But have you ever thought about how a naturalistic framework might account for such a law? How can eternal, mindless and impersonal matter produce logical laws that guide our thought?

The laws of logic flow smoothly out of a world-view that places an eternal, intelligent and personal creator as the source of all things.

On the other hand, the laws of logic flow smoothly out of a worldview that places an eternal, intelligent and personal creator as the source of all things. This underscores part of a perennial problem for the atheistic outlook. Atheists from previous generations like H.G. Wells, and even contemporary atheistic philosophers like Thomas Nagel, recognize that in atheistic naturalism there is no objective reason to trust our cognitive faculties.

Both Wells and Nagel offered these concerns in print, calling into question the bravado with which people boast of their brainpower for comprehending the world; Wells in an article, "Doubts of the Instrument," where instrument refers to the brain, and Nagel in his recent book, Mind and Cosmos: Why the Materialist Neo-Darwinian Conception of Nature Is Almost Certainly False. Both men doubt that unguided nature is able to provide a basis for cognitive confidence.

This doubt can be traced back to Charles Darwin himself, who questioned whether or not he could trust his mental thoughts if his brain is merely a product of evolution. He understood that, if nature is all there is, then there could be no certainty that our brain is reliable.

Apologists have consistently exploited this worldview weakness. C.S. Lewis claimed that this difficulty is a self-contradiction in naturalism. G.K. Chesterton called this the "thought that stops all thought."

Though much more can be said about this topic, the apologist must recognize that only Christianity provides a reasonable explanation for reason itself. Even arguments against God are forced to presuppose logical laws that only make sense if God exists. Thus, when the apologist presents the gospel, he should do so with the confidence that it is the power of God unto salvation. The gospel makes sense of the world we live in and provides a foundation for rational discussion. Truth is knowable because, as Francis Schaeffer said, "God is there and he is not silent."

2. PRESENT GOD AS SOVEREIGN

We are to present truth as knowable because of the triune God who is sovereign. If we water down our conception of God to make the gospel message more palatable we will find that, in the end, we are no longer doing true evangelism. We merely market a god of our own invention, attempting to woo people in with a hazy image of an impotent deity.

We have to remember that the people with whom we speak actually believe in God, regardless of the labels they employ. The apostle Paul makes this clear in Romans. God has revealed his invisible attributes to all men – his eternal power and his divine nature – so they are without excuse (Rom 1:19-20). The principal problem for unbelievers is that they, due to the fall, suppress the knowledge of God and worship creation rather than creator.

When we speak with unbelievers, we must keep in mind that they possess an innate knowledge of God's existence. Understanding humanity's innate knowledge of God also helps to explain the campaign against religion in our contemporary culture.

Doug Wilson said there are "two fundamental tenets of true atheism. One: there is no God. Two: I hate him." Peter Hitchens, brother of the late atheist journalist Christopher Hitchens, describes his personal conversion to Christianity in his book *The Rage Against God: How Atheism Led Me To Faith*. Peter Hitchens' conversion illustrates that belief cannot be dismissed as merely cultural. Both he and his brother rejected the faith of

> Don't dilute God in order to make him more marketable. Don't propagate idolatry. Present the sovereign God of the Bible as the key to understanding the human narrative.

their childhood. But why did Peter return, while others have continued in their rage against the God in whom they don't believe?

Paul's account in Romans 1 of man's implicit knowledge of God is telling. Just compare it to Psalm 19, which says, "The heavens declare the glory of God." What Paul writes in Romans 1 is similar, but the differences are significant. "For the wrath of God," Paul says, "is revealed from heaven." For the believer, the heavens display the glory of God.

For the unbeliever, the heavens reveal the wrath of God.

This knowledge of God brings a sense of judgment and condemnation for the unbeliever. This is a good thing. It's actually part of the divine design. That's why the cosmos is our ally in sharing with skeptics. Both physical nature and human nature point us upward. "God's kindness," Paul tells us, leads us "to repentance" (Rom 2:4). The message of the gospel is that our inner sense that there is a God, and the troubling sense that we have offended him, are both true. And it is to this point that we should direct our witness.

Don't dilute God in order to make him more marketable. Don't propagate idolatry. Present the sovereign God of the Bible as the key to understanding the human narrative.

3. PRESENT CHRIST AS SAVIOR

The human epic is stained by guilt, shame and regret. Even if some deny the reality of God, they cannot functionally deny the existence of guilt. People can try to discard it as a social construct, or repress it through medication, but there is a proven track record that emancipation from guilt can't be obtained through human efforts.

When we share the gospel with skeptics, we speak to their innate knowledge of God and their deep understanding of their moral guilt. But we must remember that guilt is only a symptom. Sin and separation from God are the true problems. And grace is the only antidote. This is why evangelism with skeptics should begin and end with a simple presentation of the gospel, and this is why the Christian apologist need not water down the gospel in order to gain a hearing. Why concede the only truth powerful enough to change hearts?

This doesn't mean the apologist should avoid responding to questions or offering arguments that force the atheist to reconsider his or her own objections. But it does mean that the apologist can never improve on Jesus' assertion, "I am the way, and the truth, and the life. No one comes to the

Evangelism with skeptics should begin and end with a simple presentation of the gospel.

Father except through me" (John 14:6). For all of your logic and all of your evidences, never abdicate your responsibility to share the good news. Our arguments cannot, in and of themselves, save anyone. Only Jesus can.

4. PRESENT SCRIPTURE AS AUTHORITATIVE

I remember my good friend Mark's quote in our senior yearbook as if it were published yesterday. Though we attended a public school, he didn't shy away from sharing his beliefs. Under his senior picture he placed this verse, "The grass withers and the flower fades but the Word of our God will stand forever" (Is 40:8).

I'm not even sure where I've stored my senior yearbook, but one thing is certain: God's Word will still remain long after my high school memorabilia is gone.

This book that you're reading will one day rot away. The paper it is printed on will deteriorate. But God's Word will not. Not only is it lasting, it is sharper than a two-edged sword (Heb 4:12). So, as you share with skeptics, don't relegate Scripture to obscurity or even to peer status among other sources. It will outlive your arguments, resources and evidences. Don't neglect, deny or seek to alter it.

You are not God's editor. You're more like a publicist. God is not waiting for your revisions. He's already gone to press.

This is not to say that every argument must be a sermon or a Bible commentary. But you should not compromise the trustworthiness of the Bible in word or attitude in order to placate a skeptic's objections. As you evangelize, you must consider where your authority is found.

If you're like most, you likely came to faith by someone opening their Bible and sharing a simple presentation of the gospel. Don't doubt that the gospel's power, on the authority of God's revelation, can do the same for those to whom you minister.

5. PRESENT MAN AS DEPRAVED

Mankind is not morally neutral. When you share the gospel, you don't speak to someone who is devoid of worldview commitments. You don't witness in a spiritual vacuum.

The Bible makes this abundantly clear. Consider Psalm 10, where the wicked says in verse five, "There is no God," and later in verse eleven, "God has forgotten, he has hidden his face, he will never see it." There is a rejection of God's existence, then, in the same breath, a fear of God's judgment. This illustrates that one's inner knowledge of God cannot be dismissed by merely proclaiming that he doesn't exist. This cognitive dissonance is as old as the Garden of Eden.

The biblical account of origins takes a tragic turn in the third chapter of Genesis. The earthly utopia of the first two chapters is merely a speed bump on the road to redemption. The rest of the biblical narrative unfolds God's plot to restore a relationship with fallen man. The biblical storyline makes no sense without an understanding of the fall. And neither will your apologetics.

Don't make the mistake of

> Sharing the gospel with skeptics is the task of shining the light of the gospel into the darkness of Satan's temporal domain.

thinking neutrality is a viable option for the unbeliever. Everyone brings a set of biases against belief in God (see Ps 10). You will encounter resistance and opposition, and this is to be expected. Stand on the Word of God and trust the gospel as the central answer for man's ultimate questions.

6. PRESENT REGENERATION AS NECESSARY

Nearly everyone I've known who is active in apologetic work deeply understands the necessity of the Spirit to bring about conversion. I've never met an apologist who sincerely believed his arguments could, in and of themselves, change someone's heart. I have, however, met many who pray fervently that God will use their meager attempts to help remove some of the intellectual obstacles. But they also pray with equal passion for the Spirit to bring about the conviction of the truthfulness of the gospel.

Sharing the gospel with skeptics is the task of shining the light of the gospel into the darkness of Satan's temporal domain. If you do it in your own power, you will fail. Like the apostle Paul, we should pray for our audience, that the eyes of their hearts might be enlightened so they might understand the truthfulness and riches of the gospel (Eph 1:18). Without the work of the Spirit, all of our work is in vain.

7. PRESENT YOURSELF AS HUMBLE

There is nothing worse than an arrogant or angry apologist, or an unnecessarily edgy evangelist. I don't care how right he or she might be; I can't stomach to watch it. The condescension is just too much.

Scripture says that we are clay pots carrying about the treasure of God's riches in Christ (2 Cor 4:7). We shouldn't take this to mean, however, that God has a low estimation of how we convey the gospel message. Superior attitudes should be remedied by taking seriously the most quoted verse in all of the Bible regarding our defense of the faith, "But in your hearts honor Christ the Lord as holy, always being prepared to make a defense to anyone who asks you for a reason for the hope that is in you; yet do it with gentleness and respect" (1 Peter 3:15). We are to present the reasons for our hope within a framework of humility.

As we present truth from a Christian basis, we point others to Jesus, the truth incarnate. When Christ is Lord, and when

> When Christ is Lord, and when we are humble, then we have found our sweet spot for doing evangelism with skeptics.

we are humble, then we have found our sweet spot for doing evangelism with skeptics. When we understand the sovereignty of God, the authority of the Bible and the necessity of the Spirit because of the fallenness of humanity, then we are well on our way to a Christ-exalting and God-glorifying approach to evangelism with atheists and agnostics.

Northern Exposure

Throughout my childhood, my family made annual trips to the beautiful Upper Peninsula of Michigan. I have fond memories of playing in the cold water of Lake Superior with my cousins. Even as an adult, I try not to let more than a couple of years go by without making a nostalgic pilgrimage to the north.

After I became a Christian at the age of fifteen, I became acutely aware of friends and family members who didn't know Christ. I remember one conversation I shared with my uncle Kevin while fishing for walleye off of his pontoon boat on Lake Michagamme. "Do you believe Jonah was really swallowed by a whale?" Kevin asked. "Uncle Kevin, I believe God created the whole world, so that's not that big of a miracle, in my opinion," I returned. It was an honest question. But I don't think Kevin was all that impressed with my answer.

Kevin has always been a great guy. But he's consistently been on the skeptical side of belief. That's why my mom sent my aunt Toni (Kevin's wife) a copy of a book filled with letters from a pastor to his skeptic father. My aunt Toni took a great interest in the book, and my uncle Kevin even became intrigued. She would often read chapters aloud on their lengthy drives across Michigan. Kevin would frequently agree with the skeptic father's concerns and questions, but he was equally impressed with the clarity of the answers that were provided.

Toward the end of the book, the father confessed his belief in God and his understanding of the life, death and resurrection of Jesus. He asked his son what he needed to do to have a relationship with God through Jesus Christ. My uncle Kevin followed in his footsteps. He repented of his sins and trusted Christ as Lord and Savior. Today, he and my aunt are active members of a small church in their community.

This story illustrates the final point I'd like to share: presenting the gospel to skeptics is a lifelong commitment. If you are out for quick conversions, or easy evangelism, then you should avoid this type of ministry. It's hard work. It will challenge your faith and often drain your soul. But like the apostle Paul at Mars Hill, though many may mock, others will stick around and inquire. And who knows, maybe the Spirit will blow in like a crisp northern wind, and some will believe (Acts 17:32-34). ∞

Resources

Further Reading

Apologetics to the Glory of God: An Introduction, John M. Frame

Christ-Centered Preaching: Redeeming the Expository Sermon, Bryan Chapell

The Church: The Gospel Made Visible, Mark Dever

Encyclopedic Dictionary of Cults, Sects, and World Religions: Revised and Updated Edition, Larry A. Nichols, George Mather, Alvin J. Schmidt

Evangelism and the Sovereignty of God, J.I. Packer

Five Views on Apologetics, Steven B. Cowan, ed.

The Gospel for Muslims: An Encouragement to Share Christ with Confidence, Thabiti Anyabwile

Mere Christianity, C.S. Lewis

The Reason for God: Belief in an Age of Skepticism, Timothy Keller

reThink, Steve Wright

A Shot of Faith (to the Head): Be a Confident Believer in an Age of Cranky Atheists, Mitch Stokes

BEVIN CENTER *for* MISSIONS MOBILIZATION

The Bevin Center for Missions Mobilization aims to train and mobilize the Southern Seminary community to be relentless in evangelism, engaged in missions and deployed in church planting from the city of Louisville to the ends of the earth. For more information, visit **missions.sbts.edu**

From Southern Seminary

Also in the Guide Book Series from SBTS Press, available at
press.sbts.edu

 *A Guide to Expository Ministry* (SBTS Press, 2012 $5.99), Dan Dumas

 *A Guide to Adoption and Orphan Care* (SBTS Press, 2012 $5.99), Russell D. Moore, Editor

 *A Guide to Biblical Manhood* (SBTS Press, 2011 $5.99), Randy Stinson and Dan Dumas

PUBLICATIONS FROM SOUTHERN SEMINARY

Southern Seminary Magazine

Towers: A News Publication of The Southern Baptist Theological Seminary

The Southern Baptist Journal of Theology

The Journal of Discipleship and Family Ministry

The Southern Baptist Journal of Missions and Evangelism

CONNECT WITH SOUTHERN SEMINARY ONLINE

News.sbts.edu
Facebook.com/TheSBTS
Twitter.com/SBTS

For more information about Southern Seminary, visit sbts.edu;
for information about Boyce College, visit boycecollege.com

Contributors

Editor

DAN DEWITT is the dean of Boyce College, the undergraduate school of The Southern Baptist Theological Seminary. He previously served as the lead pastor of Highview Baptist Church's University of Louisville Campus Church, minister to students at Judson Baptist Church in Nashville, Tenn., and associate minister to students at Highview Baptist Church. DeWitt and his wife, April, have been married for more than ten years, and are the proud parents of Isaiah, Micah, Josiah and Addilynn. DeWitt posts regularly on his blog theolatte.com

Contributors

CHAD BRAND is associate dean for biblical and theological studies and professor of Christian theology at Boyce College, where he has taught since 1999. Before coming to Louisville, Ky., he taught at North Greenville College in South Carolina. Brand is co-editor of the *Holman Illustrated Bible Dictionary* and editor of *Five Views of Church Governance* and *Perspectives on Spirit Baptism*. Brand has served as pastor of churches in Texas and as interim pastor of churches in South Carolina, Indiana and Kentucky. Brand and his wife, Tina, have three children, Tashia, Owen and Cassandra.

DENNY BURK is associate professor of biblical studies at Boyce College. Burk is the author of *Articular Infinitives in the Greek of the New Testament* and the forthcoming *What Is the Meaning of Sex?* He has also contributed to *Mounce's Complete Expository Dictionary of Old and New Testament Words* and *Don't Call It a Comeback: The Old Faith for a New Day*. He serves as editor for *The Journal for Biblical Manhood and Womanhood*, and as associate pastor at Kenwood Baptist Church in Louisville, Ky. Burk and his wife, Susan, have four children, Emily, Abby, Denny and Lucy.

TRAVIS KERNS is assistant professor of Christian worldview and apologetics at Boyce College. An expert in new religious movements, he has spoken at numerous churches and conferences dealing with the history and belief structures of the world's religions and new religious movements. Kerns is a contributing author to the forthcoming *Baker Dictionary of Cults and Sects*. His desire is to lead young men and women to have a passion for apologetics and to see persons involved in other world religions and new religious movements come to a saving knowledge of Jesus Christ. Kerns is married to Staci, and they have one son, Jeremiah.

JOHN KLAASSEN is associate professor of Christian missions at Boyce College. He is the son of missionary parents and missionary grandparents, born in Colombia, South America. Klaassen and his wife, Shari, have served with the International Mission Board since 1991, primarily in North Africa. The Klaassens, their two children and their team initiated work with three unreached people groups and helped develop a relief and development agency as a pathway for work in a restricted access nation. He completed his doctorate from Southern Seminary in 2011.

BRIAN PAYNE is assistant professor of Christian theology and expository preaching at Boyce College. He played football for the University of Alabama and then coached there as a graduate assistant. He has served in a Christian children's home, taught at a Christian high school, worked in the business world and pastored and served interim pastoral positions. Payne's desire is to teach young, aspiring pastors to be faithful in administrating and in preaching the Word of God in the local church. He also serves as senior pastor of First Baptist Church of Fisherville, Ky. Payne is married to Heather, and they have four children, Ella, Nate, Seth and Ava.

JIM STITZINGER is the director of the Bevin Center for Missions Mobilization at Southern Seminary. He previously served as a church planter and pastor in southwest Florida, and as pastor of local outreach and evangelism at Grace Community Church in Los Angeles, Calif. He contributed to *Evangelism* in the John MacArthur Pastoral Library Series and edited the Grace Evangelism training curriculum. In addition, Stitzinger served as adjunct professor of evangelism for The Master's Seminary in L.A. He and his wife, Sky, have three daughters, Macy, Jessy and Clancy.

OWEN STRACHAN is assistant professor of Christian theology and church history at Boyce College. He previously served as the managing director of the Carl F.H. Henry Center for Theological Understanding at Trinity Evangelical Divinity School in Deerfield, Ill., and the founding associate director of the Jonathan Edwards Center at TEDS. He is co-author of the five-volume *Essential Edwards Collection*, co-editor of *The Pastor as Scholar, the Scholar as Pastor: Reflections on Life and Ministry* and contributor to *Don't Call It a Comeback: The Old Faith for a New Day*. Strachan also currently serves as executive director of the Council on Biblical Manhood and Womanhood. He and his wife, Bethany, are the parents of Ella and Gavin.

TROY TEMPLE is associate professor of youth and family ministry at Southern Seminary. He has served in local church youth ministry for over two decades in Florida, Virginia, North Carolina, Kentucky and Indiana, and on the faculty and staff at Liberty University. He is actively involved in developing formal youth ministry training at seminaries in Mexico, Ukraine, Kenya, Malaysia and Nepal. He serves local church ministries by speaking to teenagers and parents, training volunteers and consulting in youth ministry. He and his wife, Karla, are the parents of Madeleine and Kathryn.

Production

PROJECT EDITOR:
MATT DAMICO is a staff writer for Southern Seminary. He earned a bachelor of arts in English from the University of Minnesota in 2008 before moving to Louisville, Ky. He graduated from Southern with a master of divinity in 2012, and currently serves as pastor of worship at Kenwood Baptist Church in Louisville. He is married to the wonderful Anna.

DESIGNER AND ILLUSTRATOR:
ANDREA STEMBER joined Southern Seminary's creative team in 2011 after working four years in the Chicago, Ill., graphic design scene. Andrea was born and raised in the state of Iowa, where she earned her bachelor of fine arts in graphic design from Iowa State University. She is married to Daniel, and they are the proud parents of Eleanor.